I0200815

Promises Made Clear

A Modern Day Catechism Companion

H. Burnell Baldwin

CSS Publishing Company, Inc., Lima, Ohio

PROMISES MADE CLEAR

Copyright © 1999 by
CSS Publishing Company, Inc.
Lima, Ohio

All rights reserved. No part of this publication may be reproduced in any manner whatsoever without the prior permission of the publisher, except in the case of brief quotations embodied in critical articles and reviews. Inquiries should be addressed to: Permissions, CSS Publishing Company, Inc., P.O. Box 4503, Lima, Ohio 45802-4503.

ISBN 0-7880-1525-7

PRINTED IN U.S.A.

Dedicated to
the memory of our son Gregory,
who was an inspiration
to those with whom he worked or played.

Table Of Contents

Preface

Luther's *Small Catechism* has long been a very useful tool in building the faith, and it has been especially so for me. In the early years of my journey with Christ I had some difficulty laying hold of the tenets of Christian faith. It is my hope and prayer that the insight and inspiration of the catechism which I have put into print will shorten the struggle that someone might have in the process of coming to grips with what we believe. This writing is an expression of my heartfelt belief and is intended to be thought-provoking for those who read it. Throughout the entire catechism I see Jesus, the author and finisher of our faith. It is Jesus I want you to see and follow faithfully as you read these words. No one else matters, for it is in Jesus that we find life that is full and abundant. The love of Jesus is beyond compare. Let him bless you.

H. Burnell Baldwin

Sacrament Of Baptism

Baptism is not simply water, but is the water with the Word.

Washing is a most ordinary event
Do it several times a day
Splashing, dipping, rubbing
To get clean
That's the main objective

The Word?
And water?
A combination of cleansers
Inside and outside
To baptize
To make clean all over

God has declared it
Made it so simple
And easy to do
Just say it with water
A child-like action
The world can understand

"Go and make disciples of all nations, baptizing them in the Name
of the Father and of the Son and of the Holy Spirit, teaching them
to observe all that I have commanded you." — Matthew 28:19-20

The water and the Word and people
Disciples the end result
God's marching orders
The mission of divine intent

Not just so many words
Or so much water
But a holy transaction
Intended for transformation
Not conformation

Learn and discern
Obedience is commanded
Else all is for nought
Not for trifling
But a lifelong follow-through
The Name is involved
God at work
Making me full of devotion

*Baptism assures forgiveness of sin, delivers from death and the
devil, and confers everlasting salvation on all who believe.*

Assurance with a plus
Not simply escape
Or a change
But a whole new life

Forgiveness wipes the slate clean
Declares holiness a gift
Overcomes death
Eradicates the devil
Ushers in an eternity of living

What kind of payment?
The death of a Son
God's Son
A baptism of defeat
Surrender
And faith claims it all
My Jesus, I love you

"Whoever believes and is baptized will be saved; but whoever does not believe will be condemned." — Mark 16:16

The simplicity of the whole transaction
Only believe
Why, everyone will go for it
It's affordable
And available
For the world

But no!
Rejection, indifference, callousness
Other things more important
God is too good to condemn
Do my own thing

The wages of sin
Unbelief the most fatal
The gift unopened
So near yet so far
Only believe
The washing is done

We were buried with Him by baptism into death, so that as Christ was raised from the dead by the glory of the Father, we too might walk in newness of life. — Romans 6:4

Death and life
Intertwined
One depends on the other
Dead to sin
Alive to God

It is a venture in faith
Open to all people
The Lord Christ the key

11

That opens the door
By death and resurrection
Vicarious atonement

The baptism of repentance
And rebirth
A whole new vista
Now and forever
I am redeemed

The Ten Commandments

I

I am the Lord your God; you shall have no other gods.

Supremacy, superiority, unrivaled
No words can suffice
No description qualifies
For the One who has no rival

Jealous for attention
And loyalty
Faith without a doubt
The objective is clear
All for One
And only One

Property, fame, intelligence
All vie for position
To unseat the author
And supplier
Of the universe

Idols can be anything
But always created
Or formed
To supplant the One
Who claims and holds Lordship

II

You shall not take the Name of the Lord your God in vain.

Reverence is a way of living
Not just words
Or avoiding words
But choosing words

Lifting up the Person
In the depths of one's soul
Honoring with the lips
And with attitude
And intent

A thankful spirit
Exuding praise and thanks
Overflowing with awareness
Of presence

Holy is the One
Whose Name spells power
Full of compassion
Willing only good
To creatures
Great and small

III

Remember the Sabbath day, to keep it holy.

Worship the Lord in spirit and truth
One is worthy
The Lord of life
And Jesus has made it known

Sunday? Saturday? Monday?
Does it matter?
Or is every day a holy day?
Created by the ruler
Of the universe

We are creatures of choice
Special in God's eyes
Clothed with the image of deity
Charged with accountability

What is our need?
A day to remember
And praise
A Word to remember
And process
Marching orders
Given especially for me

IV

Honor your father and your mother.

Parents! Guardians! Overseers!
Out from under
That's the goal
Then wisdom sets in
Age catches up
Sons and daughters
Become fathers and mothers
The cycle begins all over

The Lord is wise above all
Ordering a system
Of caring and discipline

Filling the voids
With honor and humility

Lift up the banner of family
Let the child
Learn to follow
Become a pilgrim
In the laboratory of life

V

You shall not kill.

It is life that is at stake
The creation of God Almighty
A breath of the Spirit
Filling the clay
Molded by the potter's hand

To live as fully as possible
Everyone's goal?
Not to shorten
Or cut off
With gun or knife or words
Neither chemicals or foolish acts
But lift up
With praise
Encouragement
Even self-adulation

Worthy?
I belong to God
Just like my neighbor
Beyond price
The Master's treasure

VI

You shall not commit adultery.

Faithful to the end
That's what it means
No sidelong looks
On the sly

Content because you're mine
And I am yours
God makes us one
No adulterations
Diluted
Less than honest
Not even with myself
God forbid
I want to be whole

Respect, purity, commitment
No promiscuity
The wrong kind of mixing
A twosome of divine intent
Meant to last a lifetime

VII

You shall not steal.

Honesty is the best policy
An age-old philosophy
Heard it from childhood
Essential in growing up

The law is very clear
Public or private

Property must be respected
Share the wealth
That must be the ideal

So often distribution seems faulty
Excesses and deprivations
Fairness evaporates
Temptations unfold
What's yours is mine
I'll take it

How much better
What's mine is yours
You can have it
Generous to the highest degree
Servanthood to the utmost

VIII

You shall not bear false witness against your neighbor.

Your word, my word
That's good enough
Integrity all the way through
Solid as a rock
True blue
Dependable to the end

Love one another
That's the new commandment
I am my brother's keeper
My sister's too
No one should be slighted

Boomerangs always come back
Lies can never be defended

Too much to remember
And lose
'Tis the devil's workshop
Filled with abuse

IX

You shall not covet your neighbor's house.

Be content with what you have
Wandering eyes spell trouble
Needs and wants not the same
The adrenalin flow is different

Rights and obligations
Often get mixed up
My neighbor and I
On different wave-lengths
Pretense or good intentions
Better get them straight

The value of things gets warped
Conscience runs aground
When desire takes control
Better a little with freedom
Than a slave with much

Give help and encouragement
No sweat
No self-pity
Just feeling good about me

X

You shall not covet your neighbor's wife, or his manservant, or his maidservant, or his cattle, or anything that is your neighbor's.

The eyes and the heart
A powerful team
A gut feeling
A reach that knows no bounds

Freedom within limits
So God has created
And endowed majestically
Giving to me
And to everyone
A reach beyond the grasp

The exercise of control
Placed right in front of me
I am faced with a choice
Wise or foolish
Good or bad
The outcome?
Victory or defeat
God is with me and for me
Let me be likewise

Conclusion

I the Lord your God am a jealous God, visiting the iniquity of the fathers upon the children to the third and fourth generation of those who hate me, but showing steadfast love to thousands of those who love me and keep my commandments.

Discipline and obedience
Pave the way for a good life
Parents and teachers
Employers and enforcers
Set the example

One God and only one
No rivals tolerated
None can qualify
The holy other already in charge

Let me love
With all my being
Adoration and praise
The great enablers
God is love
Who else shall I follow
Even death cannot part

The Apostles' Creed

I believe in God the Father almighty, creator of heaven and earth.

How great is our God
Who fills the universe
But has time for me
What am I?
The apple of His eye
More than a number
Worth dying for

Everything
Everyone
Is in His hands
Angels and men
Women and children
Beasts and birds
The universe boasts the Presence

All creation stands in need
Waits for redemption
Attempts to fulfill
The Creator's plans
The heavens
And the earth
Declare the glory

I believe in Jesus Christ His only Son our Lord.

The Father's secret revealed
Planned from the beginning

Declared to the prophets
Unveiled for the world

Just a baby
Entrusted to Mary
Very ordinary
But endowed with the Spirit
God's Spirit

No substitutes allowed
One and only one
A man for the masses
Identified with children
All of God's children

Call Him Lord
Teacher and friend
One for all
The Creator becomes Savior
Master of us all

He was conceived by the power of the Holy Spirit and born of the virgin Mary.

That's my Lord
Perfectly human
There is none can compare
Or compete
Just praise and adore

Magnificent!
From cradle to grave
Life to death to life
A mystery
And a reality
Hope for the world

The cradle and the cross
Of the same wood
Born to die
With a spirit immortal
Passed on to the world
For a kingdom eternal

He suffered under Pontius Pilate, was crucified, died, and was buried.

The cross
The grave
The inhumanity of the world
Focused on One

Just a nod of the head
The washing of hands
Authority and power
Gives in
Majority rules

Democracy?
Sin at its ugliest
Me?
Am I the guilty one?
Who else?
A descendant of Adam
The whole human race

He descended into hell.

What an awful thought
Could anything be worse?
The word is used every day

Downward is the movement
Nothing noble
Only extinction

Jesus did it
Made victory complete
Love conquers all
Even death
Cannot escape
Satan is outdone
The power destroyed
And life can emerge

Darkness
The realm of death
Overtaken
Defeated by life
The way and the truth
Ready to open the door

On the third day He rose from the dead.

Just like Jonah
Three days
No other sign
Then resurrection
He lives!

Miracle of miracles
Death has lost its sting
Sin's dominion gone
Life is forevermore

Jesus!
All because of Him
With perfect obedience

Father, into your hands
Trust and obey
There is no other way
One for all

He ascended into heaven.

What are dreams made of?
Hopes
Imaginations
The subconscious
Wishful thinking
It's all in the future

Ascension
Being lifted up
Encouragement is a taste
Friendship
Brotherly, sisterly love
Something to live for
Everything to hope for

Jesus is there
A place?
As near as we want it to be
More than a place
A realm
Full of love, peace, contentment
Prepared and waiting
For me!

And is seated at the right hand of the Father.

The postion of power
At the right

Supreme, eternal
No questions asked

Awesome!
God is God!
No other
Who can stand the glory?
Bow down before
King of kings
Lord of lords
Hallelujah!

The Name of Jesus
It spells dominion
Compassion and consideration
Greatness becomes a paradox
Servanthood
One for all, all for one

He will come again to judge the living and the dead.

The end of the line
No turning back
Judgment!
Acquittal or condemnation
In the hands of the Savior
The safest place to be
In Christ
No condemnation
Only salvation
From sin and death
And the devil

The King is coming
For you and me
The debt is paid

The prisoner is freed
Only believe

I believe in the Holy Spirit.

I believe
'Tis the work of the Spirit
Wonderful counselor
Persuader
Reconciler
Friend of sinners

I believe
The prompter moves me
Helps to act
And obey
There is only one way

I believe
In Jesus Christ
The gift of the Spirit
The substance
The rock of ages
Cleft for me

The holy catholic Church.

One and only one
Undivided
Universal
The body of Christ

Placed in the world
Born of the Spirit
Physical and spiritual

God's creation
Men, women, and children
One color, holy

The hands and feet of God
Prophets and priests
Servants of the Lord
Including me
And you
Baptized into Christ
United in faith
Compelled by love

The communion of saints.

Not statues
Or otherworldly
But down to earth
Ordinary
Human beings

Holy by grace
Held together
In the arms of the Spirit
A bond unbroken
But untethered
Free to burst forth

Three or thirty
Now and forever
Death has no control
This world
And the world to come
Tenants in common

The forgiveness of sins.

Heavenly transactions
Meant for all of mankind
Healing for the masses
Through one man's sacrifice

One for the sake of all
Fairness not an issue
Compassion overrides
No basis for complaint
Or excuse
God loves the world

What about relationships?
With family
And neighbors
Getting along with everyone
Hurt demands consideration
No passing the buck
I am responsible

The resurrection of the body.

The fountain of youth at last
No fairy tale guru
Not mere wishful thinking
But physical flesh and blood
In a spiritual mode

He is risen from the dead
That was the shout
Death could not hold Him
He has prepared the way
For all of us

What pleasure to behold
The end of sickness
And all infirmity

Equipped to enjoy Jesus
Good-bye to sin and death
Hello life everlasting
All in and through the Savior

Yes, Lord, I believe
Your glory to behold
And live with forever

And life everlasting. Amen.

No more death
No more sorrow
No more hoping
The miracle of life fulfilled
Ushered in with hosts of angels
And it will never end

Enjoy! Rejoice! React!
With songs of praise
I can only imagine
The glory
The fullest pleasure

Lord, your goodness overflows
No wonder time will end
It cannot be contained
No tankard is sufficient

You have filled me
Faith has turned to sight
Do I walk or jump?
For joy indescribable
Thank you, Lord Jesus

Sacrament Of The Altar

It is the true body and blood of our Lord Jesus Christ under bread and wine, given to us Christians to eat and drink, as it was instituted by Christ Himself.

Jesus of Nazareth
Of the USA too
Truly human
A gift to the whole wide world

Whoever will receive Him
Believe in His Name
Eat bread, drink the wine
A living presence is assured

Jesus said so Himself
A body spiritual
Full of substance
Given freely
To make visible, real
As promised
From eternity

The benefits of the Lord's Supper are declared in the words "given and shed for you for the forgiveness of sins."

Body beautiful
A glory to behold
Bloodied and bruised
But not broken
Pierced to the heart
And left to succumb

A gory feast
Sensation hunters come to gape
Feasting eyes on a spectacle
The object of hate

But it all backfires
With a triumphant cry
It is finished!
Forgiveness is complete
Undeserved
Offered to all of the human race

These words together with the eating and drinking are the chief things in the Sacrament.

From Adam to David to me
All-inclusive
No color or status or age denied
Come, eat and drink and live

A gift from heaven
From the Father Himself
His dearest and best
The Lord Jesus

My Savior and friend
A brother, a sister, a mother
Drink deeply
'Tis the fountain of life
Eat heartily
The bread for the world

My cup overflows
Goodness overwhelms
I melt with contrition
Lord, have mercy

Whoever believes these words and does not doubt is worthy to receive.

Is it all so simple?
Nothing to do?
Only believe?
I believe, help my unbelief
Cover my guilt
And free me to receive

Worthy Lord
And I am the worst
But you died for me
And I am washed clean

A new creation
Brought out of death
To life
Delivered
From the devil

Praise God
With all of my being
With substance
And talents
With a spirit released

A worthy celebration brings assurance of forgiveness and gives power to live a godly life.

We celebrate life
In the tasting, in the seeing
Our senses cooperate
Making real the unreal

God loves me
The cross bears witness
The blood covers the stains
Results in cleanness
Sins forgiven
A new life
Now and forever

Power from on high
A victory shout is ordered
No more hedging
Or pretending
Just walk in the light
And glorify His Name

The Lord's Prayer

Our Father who art in heaven.

Our God
A tender loving Father
Caring like no other can care
Sees every need
Hears every prayer
O my God, how great you are

Omnipresent, omniscient, omnipotent
What words can describe
Or pictures unveil
The mystery of presence
God is
Heaven is home
Earth but a footstool
Love is the word
All else fails

The Son has made the revelation
God with us
As human as we are
Yet remote as Spirit invisible
I stand in awe
Words fail
My Lord and my God always

Hallowed be thy Name.

I look up into the face of Jesus
My fears are stilled

Nerves are calmed
Rest is assured

All in a Name
The Name above every name
Representative of all that is good
Power to bring about change
And put color
And purpose
And vitality into living

Live forever and ever
That's the promise
Fulfillment rests in that Name
The Name of Jesus
One with the Father
Creator, Redeemer, Sanctifier
Nothing can compare
Or equal
It stands alone
My Lord and my God
Holy is the Name

Thy kingdom come.

God is
Where is not the question
Here, there, to the ends of the earth
The universe is God's
And the Father comes to me
In Jesus
With power
And life

Who am I?
A temple fit for God

To be filled with the Spirit
Endowed with power
Cleansed with blood
And fire

It comes to me
No effort or struggle
God's gift in Jesus
Just receive, believe
Let God come in
Make over
Resurrect
Come, Lord Jesus, come!

Thy will be done on earth as it is in heaven.

The earth is the Lord's
Heaven too
I belong to Him
No one else
God speaks
I listen
Anything else is nonsense

Nothing is too difficult
Power is given
Just let go of self
And let God be God
He leads, I follow
All the way
Heaven is my destination

I'm on the way
Short or long
It doesn't matter
God's love surrounds

Brings forth the yes in me
Belonging is everything
Kept in the center of the Master's will

Give us this day our daily bread.

Ask and it shall be given
Giving is God's business
He overflows with goodness
Generosity
Love is extravagant
God is love

Day by day
It is trust that counts
Success or failure
God is there
Providing, sustaining
Not only food and shelter
But peace and harmony
A smile, a welcome

Providence
My hands, your hands
The family is worldwide
We need each other
God makes us one
Blessed to be a blessing
Thank you, Lord, for daily bread

Forgive us our trespasses as we forgive those who trespass against us.

Lord, begin with me
The cleansing process

No one is more needy
No one is more ready
I am the guilty one

We? Us? That's me, Lord
The crowds are in need
Healing simply waits
For action
For reconciliation
But it begins with me

Trespass, iniquity, sin
It really doesn't matter
Wrong is wrong
Right is right
God is holy

Mercy falls like raindrops
Soothing, impartial, complete
Washing away the barriers
And it all begins with me

And lead us not into temptation.

The grass is greener over there
I'm missing out on something
If so many are indulging
It must be all right

Do I have the right?
Does freedom carry a license?
God has set boundaries
'Tis death to cross

Lord, take my hand
Lead me, free me

The risks are too great
Yielding is sin

The Savior is waiting
Right at the door
No excuses acceptable
The cross goes before

But deliver us from evil.

Escape! That's the cry
Somewhere to run
Away from the evil one
The wounds can be fatal

Come to me!
An urgent invite from Jesus
Open my eyes
Remove the blinders
Only believe

Prayer helps
Opens the door to the Spirit
A breath of life
Thin as a whisper
But sure as iron

A haven, a refuge
Yes, it's there
Waiting for anyone
Everyone
Just as I am

For thine is the kingdom and the power and the glory forever and ever. Amen.

Father, Son, and Holy Spirit
Picture of completeness
God for us
Us for God
Nothing is missing
Glorious

Glory to God in the highest
Forever and ever
A sinner becomes a saint
The victory bells ring
Who could plan it better

I am His, He is mine
God becomes my Savior
A happy exchange
A mutual joy
Praise the Lord, heaven rejoices

www.ingramcontent.com/pod-product-compliance
Lightning Source LLC
Chambersburg PA
CBHW071751020426
42331CB00008B/2271